School Places

by Soo Yee

NATIONAL GEOGRAPHIC

Hampton-Brown

National Geographic and the Yellow Border are registered trademarks of the National Geographic Society.

National Geographic School Publishing
Hampton-Brown
www.NGSP.com

Printed in Mexico

ISBN: 978-0-7362-7984-0

Print Number: 10   Print Year: 2020

Acknowledgments and credits continue on the inside back cover.

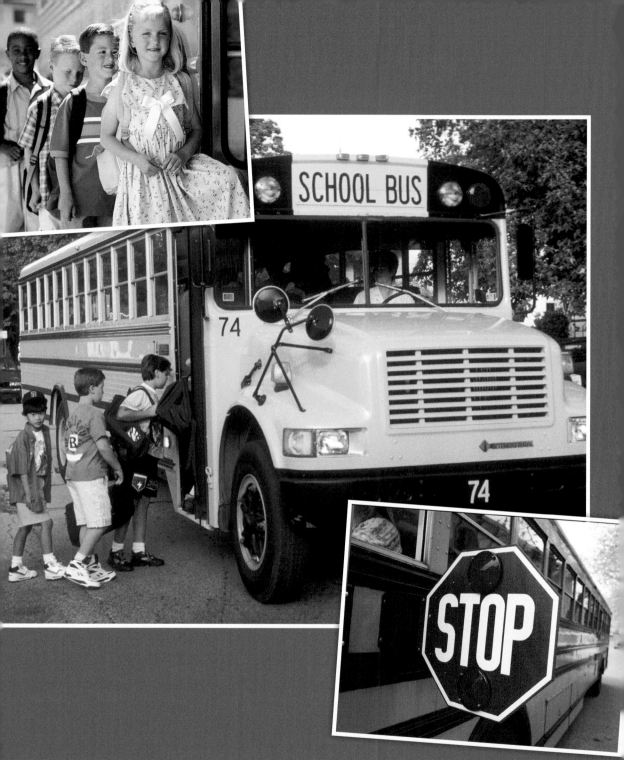

This is a bus stop.

This is a classroom.

This is a lunch room.

This is a playground.

This is a school!